Defender

 Antony Lishak

SEA-TO-SEA
Mankato Collingwood London

This edition first published in 2008 by
Sea-to-Sea Publications
1980 Lookout Drive
North Mankato
Minnesota 56003

Printed in China

Library of Congress Cataloging-in-Publication Data:

Lishak, Antony.
    Defender / by Antony Lishak.
       p.cm. (Talking about soccer)
    Includes index.
    ISBN 978-1-59771-083-1
    1. Soccer--Juvenile literature. I. Title.

GV943.25.L56 2007
796.334--dc22

                                    2006052866

9 8 7 6 5 4 3

Published by arrangement with the Watts
Publishing Group Ltd, London.

Editor: Adrian Cole
Art Director: Jonathan Hair
Design: Matthew Lilly
Cover and design concept:
Peter Scoulding

Photograph credits:
Jason Cairnduff/Prosport/
Topfoto: 6, 22.
Empics/Tofoto; 3, 8, 9, 10, 12,
14, 17, 19, 20, 21, 23, 25.
Tommy Hindley/Prosport/Topfoto:
front cover, 11, 16, 18. Jason Ison/PA/
Topfoto: 7. Keystone/Topfoto: 26, 27.
PA/Topfoto: 4, 15, 24.
Nick Potts/PA/Topfoto: 13.

Contents

⚽ What Is a Defender?

In a soccer season, the team that lets in least goals has the best chance of coming out on top. A defender's main job is to stop the other team scoring goals.

Defenders are a team's main defense. They play anywhere on the field, but they usually stay near their goal.

There are three main types of defender: central defenders, fullbacks, and wingbacks (see pages 8–9).

> "All defenders will tell you stopping goals is the most important thing in soccer."
>
> – www.bbc.co.uk/sport

▽ Defender Yourkas Seitaridis (Greece, left) closes in on Christiano Ronaldo (Portugal).

Defender Matthew Kilgallon stretches to block a cross (see page 15).

Defense

It is against the rules of soccer for defenders to touch the ball with their hands, or to push an opponent out of the way. So defenders use their feet, head, and body to stop the other side scoring a goal.

> " Moore could effortlessly steal possession from the quickest of players. "
>
> – Mike Langley, journalist

⚽ Defensive Positions

The three main types of defender work as part of the team. When the goal is under pressure from an attack, all 11 players help to defend it in different ways.

Central defender

Central defenders are also called center backs. They play just in front of their penalty area in the center of the field. Central defenders do not usually take part in an attack, unless it is from a corner or free kick (see pages 24–25). The Danish captain Thomas Helveg is a central defender.

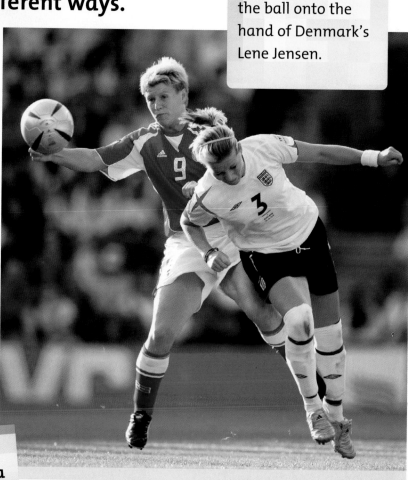

▽ England's fullback Rachel Unitt heads the ball onto the hand of Denmark's Lene Jensen.

> " The best central defenders have to be a tower of strength, great in the tackle and in the air, and sound on the ball. "
>
> – www.manchester online.co.uk

Fullback

A fullback plays either side of the central defenders. A fullback, such as England's Rachel Unitt, passes the ball to strikers and takes part in some attacks.

Wingback

A wingback does the same job as a fullback, but runs along the side of the field, called the "wing." They help the team attack, make crosses into the strikers, and may even run with the ball to score themselves. Celestine Babayaro, a Nigerian player, often plays in a wingback position.

▷ Celestine Babayaro lines up in defense for Nigeria.

▷ HALL OF FAME

Aged 16 years, Celestine Babayaro became the youngest player to play in the Champions League. He made his international debut for Nigeria a year later and won an Olympic gold medal with the team at the 1996 Atlanta Olympics.

" Babayaro excels in man-to-man marking and couples that with surges up the wing, adding a further attacking option. "

– www.news.bbc.co.uk

Team Play

Soccer is a team sport. Often, a team wins a game by working together and playing well, not just by having the most skillful players. Defenders work as a group to provide the strongest defense.

▷ Anderlecht's Vincent Kompany and Lamine Traore challenge Inter Milan's Adriano for the ball.

Covering gaps

It is important for defenders to stay alert. If one of their teammates moves forward with the ball they must change their position. This covers any empty space and stops the other team scoring easily.

> " When you get hold of the ball, stay calm. When your team is under pressure, keeping possession is perfect for taking the sting out of the game. "
>
> – Faye White, England defender

Communication

It's quite common for the team captain to be a central defender. He or she has a clear view of everything. They can call out instructions when they are needed. All the players also talk or call to each other during a game.

▽ Teng Wei of China covers for her teammate with a challenge on Birgit Prinz of Germany.

▷ SKILLS TIPS

• When you have control of the ball, keep your head up and look for teammates who could receive a pass.
• If a player from your team has the ball, be prepared to receive a pass from them.
• Help forward players by moving toward the opposition's goal during an attack.

Offside

Offside is when an opponent goes behind the line of defenders before the ball is kicked forward to them. When this happens the game stops and a free kick is awarded. If all the defenders work together they can "trap" a player offside.

❝ Nothing comes above the team, this is the first rule. You can't just do your own thing. You have to run the tactics that you have agreed otherwise you cannot play your game. ❞

– Otto Rehhagel, who coached Greece to victory at Euro 2004

Staying in Shape

Soccer players need to be in good shape.
That means they need to eat the right
food and do exercise and training.

△
Nick Garcia takes a drink during
a break in a soccer game.

> **Great players look
> after themselves and
> their superb fitness allows
> them to cover virtually
> every blade of grass from
> the middle of the field to
> all the corners.**
>
> **– Keith Anderson,
> journalist**

Food and water

Food gives soccer players the
energy they need to play well.
They eat a balanced diet. Food
such as potatoes provides them
with carbohydrates. Fish and
beans provide them with
protein, and fresh fruit and
vegetables provide minerals
and vitamins. It is also
important for players to drink
plenty of water. They must
replace the water they sweat
when they exercise.

Lauren keeps pace with Dennis Bergkamp during an Arsenal training session.

> **Many defenders are good on the ball but they need to be hard as nails as well.**
>
> – observer.guardian.co.uk

Exercise and training

A soccer match usually lasts for 90 minutes (although games for younger players are often shorter). A defender requires stamina and strength to play for a whole game, so all soccer players train regularly. Before every training session they "warm up" by stretching their muscles. During a session they lift weights in a gym to build up their muscle strength. On other days they may run long distances to build up their stamina.

⚽ Tackling

One of the most important jobs a defender has is to take the ball away from the other team's strikers. Defenders must try to win the ball back with their feet. This is called tackling.

A clean tackle

To make a successful tackle it is important that defenders only kick the ball. This is called a clean tackle. If a defender kicks an opponent's leg, instead of the ball, it is a foul. The other team is given a free kick.

⚠ It is important for defenders to make a clean tackle like this. It could stop a striker scoring a goal.

> ❝ Keep the attacker under pressure and wait for the best opportunity to make a tackle. ❞
>
> – Katie Chapman, England defender

A block tackle

Defenders use a block tackle when a striker is about to shoot at goal. They block the ball with their body or leg. The ball might hurt when it hits them, but defenders would rather have a bruised leg than let the other side score a goal.

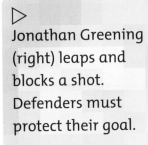

▷ Jonathan Greening (right) leaps and blocks a shot. Defenders must protect their goal.

> A well timed tackle, like a goal, can be the difference between victory and defeat.
>
> – Dave Smith, coach

Timing the tackle

A defender has to time a tackle correctly. If a tackle is too early, the striker will move the ball out of the way. If it is too late, the striker will kick the ball past the defender. A badly timed tackle could foul the other player. If this happens in the penalty area, they are given a free kick at goal, called a penalty kick. This is a good chance to score.

⚽ Marking

Defenders are often told by their manager which particular strikers to mark. When marking a player, a defender stays close to him or her. This makes it more difficult for the striker to shoot or pass the ball.

A defender can easily stop a pass reaching the striker when they are marking them. This is called intercepting the ball. Marking the striker also makes it difficult for him or her to control the ball. It puts the striker under more pressure.

> ❝ Players will get frustrated by man-to-man marking, no matter what sort of player they are. ❞
>
> – Paul Robinson, defender

▷ Brazil's Roberto Carlos (left) closely marks Patrick Vieira of France. He makes sure he is in a position to intercept the ball.

Marking space

Sometimes, defenders are told to mark part of the field. This helps to prevent the other team from attacking. But they must stay aware of what their opponents are doing. A defender must be ready to respond to different attacks; otherwise a striker might score a goal while the defender is still in an empty part of the field!

△
The three players (circled) are holding a strong defensive line. But they are still watching the game and responding to an attack.

" The problem with [marking space] is that because of the movement of the opposition, you're going to have players that are unmarked. "

– Alan Hansen, former Liverpool defender

Clearing the Ball

A defender can make lots of great tackles, but it only takes one error for a striker to get past and score a goal. Defenders clear the ball by kicking or heading it away from their goal.

▷ Cat Reddick of the USA chases down Cristiane of Brazil who is attacking quickly.

Kicking it out

A game of soccer can be very fast. Players might have only a split second to decide what to do. When a defender is under pressure from a quick attack, it's better to kick the ball off the field, or "into touch." This stops the game and gives the rest of the defenders time to get into position to protect their goal.

" I never want to settle for where I am because there's always room to improve. Learning and watching the game is what's going to do that for me. "

– Cat Reddick, USA women's international

◁ Rising to head the ball clear. A clearing header is directed away from the goal.

A clearing header

Defenders can stop some attacks with a clearing header. They direct the ball toward one of their own players or just away from the goal. Tall central defenders, such as John Terry (England) and Sylvain Distin (France), are especially good at heading the ball. It takes courage for a defender to challenge for a ball with their head, but if they don't, a striker could score a goal.

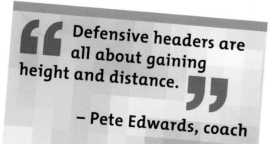

" Defensive headers are all about gaining height and distance. "

– Pete Edwards, coach

SKILLS TIPS

- When under pressure to clear the ball, make a decision quickly. If you have to clear the ball in the penalty area, try to kick the ball toward the other team's goal.
- Concentrate on kicking, or making good contact, with the ball.
- Don't pass the ball across your own penalty area unless you have lots of time.

Moving the Ball

Defenders mainly stop the other side scoring a goal. But when a defender has the ball, and there are no opponents nearby, they have the chance to start an attack for their own team.

> " The moment a defender wins the ball there is a golden opportunity for a counter attack. "
>
> – Charles Hughes, coach

Sandra Minnert breaks from defense for Germany. But she has fouled a Brazilian player, and wasted a chance to attack.

Accurate passing

Passing a ball accurately is an important soccer skill. A good pass can create a chance for the team to attack. Defenders pass the ball carefully. If the pass is hit too hard, the ball might go into touch. If it's too soft, it might not even get to the right player! Long passes from defense can also start a quick attack.

England's Rachel Unitt starts an attack by bringing the ball out of defense.

> " Quite simply, attack is what happens whenever your team has the ball and defense is what happens whenever the opposing team has the ball. "
>
> – www.avrosport.co.uk

Bringing the ball out

Most defenders don't attack by running with the ball at their feet. The midfield players and strikers are usually better at doing that. But sometimes a defender brings the ball out of defense and moves into the other team's half of the field. Defenders can surprise their opponents when they do this, and create a scoring chance for the strikers.

Wing Play

The wings are the sides of the field nearest the touchlines. Some teams have defenders called wingbacks, who run along these areas to attack. This is a highly skilled job that requires a huge amount of energy.

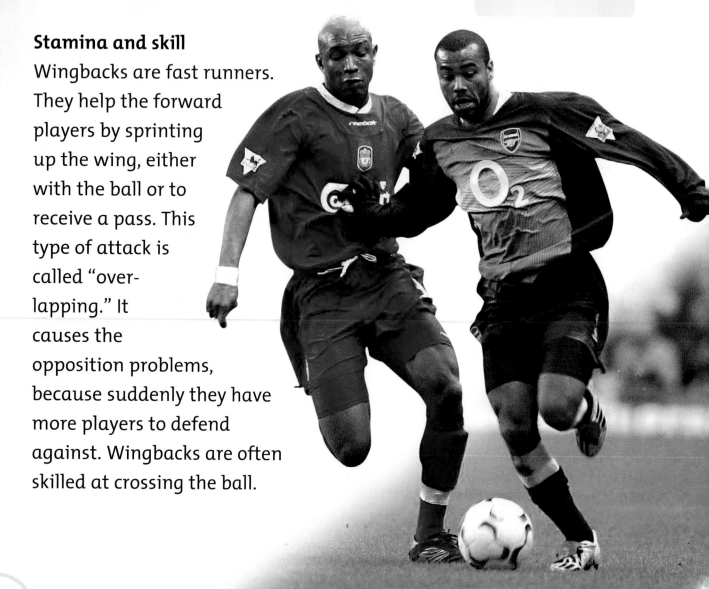

Arsenal and England wingback Ashley Cole (right) sprints down the left wing while controlling the ball.

Stamina and skill

Wingbacks are fast runners. They help the forward players by sprinting up the wing, either with the ball or to receive a pass. This type of attack is called "over-lapping." It causes the opposition problems, because suddenly they have more players to defend against. Wingbacks are often skilled at crossing the ball.

Tracking back into defense. It is important to get back into position quickly because the opposition could start an attack.

Tracking back

When a wingback sprints forward, the gap they leave in the defense is usually filled by a central defender. But if the attack is stopped and the other side win possession of the ball, the wingback must return to the defense quickly. This is called tracking back.

▷ HALL OF FAME

Faye White is the Arsenal and England women's captain. She is a powerful central defender and has won 16 major trophies in her nine years at Arsenal. She has played 48 international games, first joining the squad when she was 17.

> Faye White is one of the stars of the women's game—how many Premiership defenders send "rasping drives" flying into the net from 30 meters out?

> – Mark Crellin , journalist

⚽ Setpieces

Games of soccer are usually fast. Sportscasters call them "end-to-end" games. But even these matches stop for corners and free kicks. These are called setpieces. Teams spend time practicing them during training.

▷ Shooting at goal after a corner kick. In these situations a defender often needs to make a blocking tackle.

Getting into position

Players who take corners and free kicks usually wait for their teammates to get into position. These moments also allow defenders to get ready for an attack.

A defensive wall

When the opposition has a free kick within shooting range, the defending team forms a defensive wall. Players make a human barrier between the ball and the goal. It is important that the wall stays together. If a ball flies through a gap it could surprise the goalkeeper and may go into the goal.

△
A Dynamo Kiev defensive wall. Maksim Shatskikh looks over his shoulder to follow his goalkeeper's directions.

A chance to score

Setpieces also provide a great opportunity for defenders to score goals in attack. Usually, at least one defender goes into the opposition's penalty area for a corner or free kick.

Study the Stars

There are lots of chances for young players to watch their favorite defenders on television. But it is even better to go and watch a live game. Then you can see all the movements the defense makes.

▽
Hertha Berlin fans enjoy watching their team in Germany.

> The art of good defending takes a disciplined mind and body and all players should be taught how to do it properly.
>
> – Wayne Harrison, coach and author

Deciding your best position

Young defenders should ask themselves certain questions about their abilities. Are you right- or left-footed? Can you run fast? Are you strong and tall so you can head the ball well? Can you pass the ball well? These questions will help you decide on the defensive position that suits you.

Trying things out

The best way to enjoy soccer is to play it. Many young players start off by joining a local team, or by playing for the school team. Keep practicing your blocking, tackling, and heading skills so that you gradually improve your defending.

A television camera at a football game. Many European and international soccer games are shown on cable and satellite TV.

Following the dream

Many teams have training schemes for young players. With hard work and practice some players become professional defenders. Remember, soccer is a great game, whatever level you play it at.

HALL OF FAME

The Real Madrid defender and Brazilian international, Roberto Carlos, is considered to be one of the best defenders in the world. As well as having great speed, he is well known for scoring from long-distance free kicks.

⚽ Web Sites

www.givemefootball.com/coaching
The official site of the UK's Professional Footballers' Association. It includes lots of skills tips under the "improve your game" section.

www.footballasia.com
This web site includes information about all the Asian soccer competitions, including ones for women.

www.footballaustralia.com.au
The official web site of Football Federation Australia. Find out more about the national team and Australians playing soccer all round the world.

www.bobbymooreonline.co.uk
Find out all there is to know about the captain of the 1966 England World Cup winning side.

www.uefa.com
Europe's soccer web site for news and details of all the current competitions, including player profiles and an online magazine.

www.fifa.com
Official web site of the Fédération Internationale de Football Association. It features football news and history.

www.ussoccer.com
Home of the US Soccer Federation. This web site includes US soccer team information, the history of US soccer, and the laws of the game.

Every effort has been made by the Publishers to ensure that these web sites contain no inappropriate or offensive material. However, because of the nature of the Internet, it is impossible to guarantee that the contents of these sites will not be altered. We strongly advise that Internet access is supervised by a responsible adult.

 Glossary

Block tackle
– when a defender uses his or her body or leg to stop an opponent moving the ball.

Carbohydrates
– parts of food that contain energy.

Challenge
– to tackle a member of the other team.

Cross
– sending the ball from the sideline to the center of the field, usually into the other team's penalty area.

Energy
– what a player needs to play soccer well.

Foul
– to break one of the rules.

Free kick
– how a team restarts the game after a foul.

Intercepting
– cutting off a pass between two opponents.

Midfield
– the part of the field nearest the halfway line.

Minerals
– parts of food that keep the body healthy.

Opponent
– a player from the team you are playing against.

Penalty area
– the large box area that is shown by a white line in front of the goal.

Penalty kick
– a special free kick awarded when a foul has been committed in the penalty area.

Possession
– when a team has control of the ball.

Pressure
– when one team tries hard to regain possession.

Professional
– being paid a wage to play football.

Protein
– a part of food that keeps you healthy.

Sportscaster
– someone who explains what is happening when a game is televised.

Sprint
– to run very fast.

Stamina
– the ability to run and work hard for long periods.

⚽ Index